WHSmith

Revision

Maths

Paul Broadbent and
Peter Patilla

**Age 8–9
Year 4
Key Stage 2**

Hachette UK's policy is to use papers that are natural, renewable and recyclable products and made from wood grown in sustainable forests. The logging and manufacturing processes are expected to conform to the environmental regulations of the country of origin.

Orders: please contact Bookpoint Ltd, 130 Milton Park, Abingdon, Oxon OX14 4SB. Telephone: (44) 01235 827720. Fax: (44) 01235 400454. Lines are open 9.00a.m.–5.00p.m., Monday to Saturday, with a 24-hour message answering service. Visit our website at www.hoddereducation.co.uk.

© Paul Broadbent and Peter Patilla 2013
First published in 2007 exclusively for WHSmith by
Hodder Education
An Hachette UK Company
Carmelite House
50 Victoria Embankment
London EC4Y 0DZ
This second edition first published in 2013 exclusively for WHSmith by Hodder Education.

Impression number   10 9 8 7 6 5 4 3
Year   2018

This edition has been updated, 2014, to reflect National Curriculum changes.

All rights reserved. Apart from any use permitted under UK copyright law, no part of this publication may be reproduced or transmitted in any form or by any means, electronic or mechanical, including photocopying and recording, or held within any information storage and retrieval system, without permission in writing from the publisher or under licence from the Copyright Licensing Agency Limited. Further details of such licences (for reprographic reproduction) may be obtained from the Copyright Licensing Agency Limited, Saffron House, 6–10 Kirby Street, London EC1N 8TS.

Cover illustration by Oxford Designers and Illustrators Ltd
All other illustrations by Fakenham Prepress Solutions, Fakenham, Norfolk NR21 8NN
Typeset in 16pt Folio by Fakenham Prepress Solutions, Fakenham, Norfolk NR21 8NN
Printed in Italy

A catalogue record for this title is available from the British Library.

ISBN: 978 1444 189 032

Contents

Unit 1	Place value	**6**
Unit 2	Digits	**7**
Unit 3	Sequences	**8**
Unit 4	Patterns on grids	**9**
Unit 5	Comparing numbers	**10**
Unit 6	Ordering numbers	**11**
Unit 7	Odd and even numbers	**12**
Unit 8	Multiples	**13**
Unit 9	Fractions	**14**
Unit 10	Equivalent fractions	**15**
Unit 11	Addition and subtraction facts	**16**
Unit 12	Function machines	**17**
Unit 13	Mental addition	**18**
Unit 14	Addition patterns	**19**
Unit 15	Finding the difference	**20**
Unit 16	Mental subtraction	**21**
Unit 17	Using brackets	**22**
Unit 18	Multiplication facts	**23**
Unit 19	Doubling	**24**
Unit 20	Mixed calculations	**25**
Unit 21	Division	**26**
Unit 22	Division and remainders	**27**
Unit 23	Money	**28**
Unit 24	Money calculations	**29**
Unit 25	Mixed problems	**30**

Unit 26	Mixed puzzles	**31**
Unit 27	2D shapes	**32**
Unit 28	Symmetry	**33**
Unit 29	Naming 3D solids	**34**
Unit 30	Properties of 3D solids	**35**
Unit 31	Angles	**36**
Unit 32	Coordinates	**37**
Unit 33	Measuring length	**38**
Unit 34	Measuring mass	**39**
Unit 35	Measuring capacity	**40**
Unit 36	Perimeter	**41**
Unit 37	Time	**42**
Unit 38	Calendars	**43**
Unit 39	Pictograms	**44**
Unit 40	Bar charts	**45**
	Test 1	**46**
	Test 2	**48**
	Test 3	**50**
	Test 4	**52**
	Parents' notes	**54**
	Answers	**58**

The *WHS Revision* series

The *WHS Revision* books enable you to help your child revise and practise important skills taught in school. These skills form part of the National Curriculum and will help your child to improve his or her Maths and English.

Testing in schools

During their time at school all children will undergo a variety of tests. Regular testing is a feature of all schools. It is carried out:

- *informally* – in everyday classroom activities your child's teacher is continually assessing and observing your child's performance in a general way
- *formally* – more regular formal testing helps the teacher check your child's progress in specific areas.

Testing is important because:

- it provides evidence of your child's achievement and progress
- it helps the teacher decide which skills to focus on with your child
- it helps compare how different children are progressing.

The importance of revision

Regular revision is important to ensure your child remembers and practises skills he or she has been taught. These books will help your child revise and test his or her knowledge of some of the things he or she will be expected to know. They will help you prepare your child to be in a better position to face tests in school with confidence.

How to use this book

Units

This book is divided into forty units, each focusing on one key skill. Each unit begins with a **Remember** section, which introduces and revises essential information about the particular skill covered. If possible, read and discuss this with your child to ensure he or she understands it.

This is followed by a **Have a go** section, which contains a number of activities to help your child revise the topic thoroughly and use the skill effectively. Usually, your child should be able to do these activities fairly independently.

Revision tests

There are four revision tests in the book (pages 46–53). These test the skills covered in the preceding units and assess your child's progress and understanding. They can be marked by you or by your child. Your child should fill in his or her test score for each test in the space provided. This will provide a visual record of your child's progress and an instant sense of confidence and achievement.

Parents' notes

The parents' notes (on pages 54–57) provide you with brief information on each skill and explain why it is important.

Answers

Answers to the unit questions and tests may be found on pages 58–64.

5

Unit 1: Place value

● Remember

The numbers between 1000 and 9999 all have **four digits**.
The position of a digit in a number gives it a **value**.

4835 = 4000 + 800 + 30 + 5

● Have a go

1 Write the missing numbers.

a 4362 → 4000 + 300 + 60 + 2   b 2145 → 2000 + 100 + 40 + 5

c 6714 → 6000 + 700 + 10 + 4   d 3977 → 3000 + 900 + 70 + 7

e 1234 → 1000 + 200 + 30 + 4   f 2821 → 2000 + 800 + 20 + 1

g 3285 → 3000 + 200 + 80 + 5   h 9376 → 9000 + 300 + 70 + 6

2 Complete this number puzzle.

Across
1. Six thousand one hundred and ninety-three
3. Three thousand two hundred and eight
4. One thousand seven hundred and ninety-four
6. Three thousand nine hundred and twenty-three

Down
1. Six thousand eight hundred and four
2. Nine thousand four hundred
4. One thousand and forty-three
5. Nine thousand three hundred and fifty-two

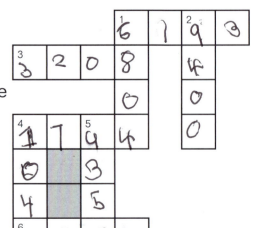

Unit 2: Digits

Remember

The numbers between 1000 and 9999 all have **four digits**:
thousands, **hundreds**, **tens** and **ones**.

When you add or subtract 1, 10, 100 or 1000, the digits are changed:

4273 + **1** = 4274
4273 + **10** = 4283
4273 + **100** = 4373
4273 + **1000** = 5273

Have a go

1 Continue these counting chains.

a 1895 → + 1 → 1896 → + 1 → 1897 → + 1 → 1898 → + 1 → 1899

b 6048 → − 1 → 6044 6047 → − 1 → 6050 6046 → − 1 → 6051 6045 → − 1 → 6052 6044

c 3184 → + 10 → 3194 → + 10 → 3204 → + 10 → 3214 → + 10 → 3224

d 2653 → − 10 → 2643 → − 10 → 2632 → − 10 → 2622 → − 10 → 2612

2

a 3659 → + 100 → 3759 → + 100 → 3851 3859 → + 100 → 3951 3959 → + 100 → 4059

b 5278 → − 100 → 5178 → − 100 → 5018 → − 100 → 4478 → − 100 → 4878

c 2093 → + 1000 → 3093 → + 1000 → 4093 → + 1000 → 5093 → + 1000 → 6093

d 7928 → − 1000 → 6928 → − 1000 → 5928 → − 1000 → 4928 → − 1000 → 3928

Unit 3: Sequences

Remember

To work out the **pattern** in a **sequence**, look at the **difference** between each number.

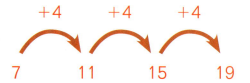

The pattern or rule is +4.

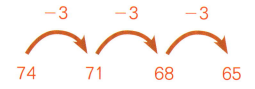

The pattern or rule is −3.

Have a go

1 Continue these sequences and write the rule.

a 18 23 28 33 37 41 45 49
Rule: +4

b 41 39 37 35 32 29 26 23
Rule: −3

c 54 57 60 63 67 71 75 79
Rule: +4

d 38 42 46 50 47 46 41 38
Rule: −3

e 94 84 74 64 68 72 76 80
Rule: +4

f 87 82 77 72 69 66 63 60
Rule: −3

2 Write the missing numbers.

a 150 200 250 300 350 400
b 350 400 375 350 325 300
c 1010 910 810 710 610 510
d 200 225 250 275 300 325

Unit 4: Patterns on grids

Remember

You can see **patterns of sequences** on grids.
This sequence shows a pattern of threes. The numbers start at three and count on in threes. Look for the different patterns.

1	2	3	4	5
6	7	8	9	10
11	12	13	14	15
16	17	18	19	20
21	22	23	24	25

Have a go

1 Shade in the numbers following these rules:

a Start at two and count on in threes.

1	2	3	4	5
6	7	8	9	10
11	12	13	14	15
16	17	18	19	20
21	22	23	24	25

Circle the number that would be in your sequence: 27 31 35

b Start at two and count on in fours.

1	2	3	4	5
6	7	8	9	10
11	12	13	14	15
16	17	18	19	20
21	22	23	24	25

Circle the number that would be in your sequence: 32 36 38

c Start at three and count on in fours.

1	2	3	4	5	6
7	8	9	10	11	12
13	14	15	16	17	18
19	20	21	22	23	24
25	26	27	28	29	30
31	32	33	34	35	36

Circle the number that would be in your sequence: 40 43 49

d Start at one and count on in threes.

1	2	3	4	5	6
7	8	9	10	11	12
13	14	15	16	17	18
19	20	21	22	23	24
25	26	27	28	29	30
31	32	33	34	35	36

Circle the number that would be in your sequence: 40 42 50

2 Look at the patterns you can make on this grid.

1	2	3	4	5	6	7
8	9	10	11	12	13	14
15	16	17	18	19	20	21
22	23	24	25	26	27	28
29	30	31	32	33	34	35
36	37	38	39	40	41	42
43	44	45	46	47	48	49

Start at any number. What are the patterns formed if you:
- count in threes?
- count in fours?
- count in fives?
- count in eights?

Shade the squares to show your favourite pattern.

Unit 5: Comparing numbers

Remember

You use < and > to compare numbers.
< means **is less than**
For example, 385 < 390.
385 is less than 390.

> means **is greater than**
For example, 821 > 812.
821 is greater than 812.

Have a go

1 Write the signs < or > for each pair of numbers.

a 348 ☐ 426   b 514 ☐ 541   c 806 ☐ 805
d 517 ☐ 509   e 934 ☐ 919   f 2453 ☐ 2540
g 1800 ☐ 1796   h 4975 ☐ 4957   i 7604 ☐ 7640

2 Write the signs < or > for these.

a 4618 ☐ 4068 ☐ 4608   b 2007 ☐ 2070 ☐ 2700
c 3274 ☐ 3280 ☐ 3278   d 4283 ☐ 4238 ☐ 4240
e 2977 ☐ 2980 ☐ 2897   f 7035 ☐ 7028 ☐ 7019

3 Solve these problems.

a 2946 < ☐ < 2952

Which numbers could be in the empty box?

_____

b 4811 > ☐ > 4807

Which numbers could be in the empty box?

_____

Unit 6: Ordering numbers

Remember

You often need to put **lists of numbers** in order of size.
To help work out the order you can write them down in a column, lining up the units.

4874   4087   4874   497   89

4874
4087
497
89

Compare each digit, starting with the thousands column.

Have a go

1. Write these numbers in order, starting with the smallest.

a) 595   2005   529   2509   2053   _____ _____ _____ _____ _____

b) 2681   2068   1023   988   1009   _____ _____ _____ _____ _____

c) 4037   4307   3740   4730   4703   _____ _____ _____ _____ _____

d) 2911   3006   299   2894   2990   _____ _____ _____ _____ _____

e) 3452   6112   3098   1665   6121   _____ _____ _____ _____ _____

2. Use the digits 4, 5, 8, 3.

Make as many different 4-digit numbers as you can.
Write them in order, starting with the smallest.

Unit 7: Odd and even numbers

Remember

All **even numbers** can be divided exactly by 2.
They always end in 0, 2, 4, 6 or 8.

All **odd numbers** cannot be divided exactly by 2.
They always end in 1, 3, 5, 7 or 9.

Have a go

1 Colour all the odd numbers in this grid.

86	104	92	268	308	676	204
34	61	125	73	74	95	156
100	216	110	221	62	639	98
94	723	319	505	312	487	6
72	491	198	716	4	189	58
418	607	47	183	232	215	220
636	142	30	22	412	906	134

What is the hidden number? ☐

2 Write the missing numbers.

a 137   139   ☐   143   ☐   147

b 206   208   210   ☐   ☐   216

c ☐   443   ☐   439   437   ☐

d 808   806   ☐   802   ☐   ☐

3 Test these out with different numbers. Tick the ones that are true.

a odd number + odd number ⟶ always makes an even number? ☐

b odd number − odd number ⟶ always makes an odd number? ☐

c even number − odd number ⟶ always makes an even number? ☐

d even number + odd number ⟶ always makes an odd number? ☐

e even number − even number ⟶ always makes an even number? ☐

f even number + even number ⟶ always makes an odd number? ☐

Unit 8: Multiples

Remember

Multiples are like the numbers in the times tables, but they go on and on.

Multiples of 2 are: 2, 4, 6, 8, 10, 12, . . ., 52, 54, 56 and so on.
Multiples of 5 are: 5, 10, 15, 20, 25, . . ., 75, 80, 85 and so on.
Multiples of 10 are: 10, 20, 30, 40, 50, . . ., 140, 150, 160 and so on.
Multiples of 25 are: 25, 50, 75, 100, 125, . . ., 250, 275, 300 and so on.

Have a go

1 Look at these numbers.
Write them in the correct boxes.
Be careful – some will be in more than one box.

74 225 60 92 35 150 88 95 130 28 45 90 36 75

multiples of 2	multiples of 5	multiples of 10

Write the numbers that are multiples of 2, 5 and 10 from the list above:

2

1	2	3	4	5	6	7	8	9	10
11	12	13	14	15	16	17	18	19	20
21	22	23	24	25	26	27	28	29	30
31	32	33	34	35	36	37	38	39	40
41	42	43	44	45	46	47	48	49	50
51	52	53	54	55	56	57	58	59	60
61	62	63	64	65	66	67	68	69	70
71	72	73	74	75	76	77	78	79	80
81	82	83	84	85	86	87	88	89	90
91	92	93	94	95	96	97	98	99	100

a Colour all the multiples of 2.

b Circle all the multiples of 5.

c What do you notice about the multiples of 10?

13

Unit 9: Fractions

⬤ Remember

Fractions have a **numerator** and a **denominator**.

$$\text{numerator} \rightarrow \frac{3}{4} \leftarrow \text{denominator}$$

The denominator shows the number of equal parts.
The numerator shows how many of them are needed.
When you add fractions with the same denominator you just add the numerators.

$$\frac{1}{4} + \frac{3}{4} = \frac{4}{4} = 1$$

When you subtract fractions with the same denominator you just subtract the numerators.

$$\frac{5}{6} - \frac{1}{6} = \frac{4}{6}$$

⬤ Have a go

1 What fraction of each of these is shaded blue?

a    b   c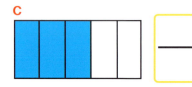

d 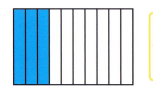   e   f

2 Use the pictures above to help you answer these.

a $\frac{1}{3} + \frac{1}{3} =$ b $\frac{7}{10} - \frac{3}{10} =$ c $\frac{3}{5} + \frac{2}{5} =$

d $\frac{9}{10} - \frac{3}{10} =$ e $\frac{3}{8} + \frac{1}{8} =$ f $\frac{4}{5} - \frac{3}{5} =$

Unit 10: Equivalent fractions

Remember

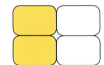

Some fractions are worth the same if the numerators and denominators are different.

These are called **equivalent fractions**.

Have a go

1. What fraction of each of these is shaded red?
   Write each fraction in two ways.

a $\frac{1}{\square} = \frac{\square}{8}$

b 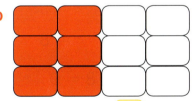 $\frac{1}{\square} = \frac{\square}{12}$

c  $\frac{1}{\square} = \frac{\square}{6}$

d  $\frac{3}{\square} = \frac{\square}{8}$

e $\frac{1}{\square} = \frac{\square}{10}$

f $\frac{1}{\square} = \frac{\square}{12}$

2. Continue these equivalent fraction chains.

a $\frac{1}{2} = \frac{2}{\square} = \frac{3}{\square} = \frac{\square}{8} = \frac{\square}{10} = \frac{6}{\square}$

b $\frac{1}{3} = \frac{2}{\square} = \frac{\square}{9} = \frac{4}{\square} = \frac{5}{\square} = \frac{\square}{18}$

c $\frac{1}{4} = \frac{2}{\square} = \frac{3}{\square} = \frac{4}{\square} = \frac{5}{20} = \frac{6}{\square}$

d $\frac{1}{5} = \frac{\square}{10} = \frac{3}{\square} = \frac{\square}{20} = \frac{5}{\square} = \frac{6}{\square}$

15

Unit 11: Addition and subtraction facts

⬤ Remember

If you know your **addition facts**, it can help you learn your **subtraction facts**.

For example, the trio 4, 8 and 12 can make four facts:
4 + 8 = 12
8 + 4 = 12
12 − 4 = 8
12 − 8 = 4

⬤ Have a go

1 Write the four facts for each of these 'trios'.

a
6 + ☐ = ☐
☐ + 6 = 14
☐ − 8 = 6
14 − ☐ = 8

(trio: 6, 8, 14)

b
☐ + 9 = 17
9 + ☐ = ☐
17 − ☐ = 8
☐ − 8 = 9

(trio: 8, 9, 17)

c
6 + ☐ = ☐
☐ + 6 = 9
☐ − 3 = 6
9 − ☐ = 3

(trio: 3, 6, 9)

d
☐ + 7 = 12
7 + ☐ = ☐
12 − ☐ = 5
☐ − 5 = ☐

(trio: 5, 7, 12)

2 Use a timer. Answer these as quickly as you can.

a 4+7 = ☐   b 9+4 = ☐   c 8+8 = ☐   d 6+5 = ☐

e 7+6 = ☐   f 5+8 = ☐   g 16−7 = ☐   h 15−8 = ☐

i 19−8 = ☐   j 11−8 = ☐   k 18−9 = ☐   l 15−6 = ☐

Try it again. Can you beat your best time?

16

Unit 12: Function machines

● Remember

Addition and **subtraction** are opposites.

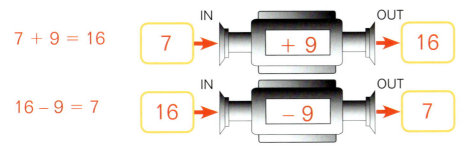

$7 + 9 = 16$

$16 - 9 = 7$

● Have a go

1 Write the missing numbers for each machine.

a

IN	7		11		14	
OUT		12		20		17

b

IN		5		8	15	
OUT		15		21		18

c

IN	14		18		15	
OUT		8		5		14

d

IN	20		17		25	
OUT		6		12		14

2 This is a two-part machine. Write the missing numbers.

IN	6		18		12	
OUT		14		9		1

17

Unit 13: Mental addition

● Remember

When you **add** two numbers in your head, there are many different methods you can use. How would you work out 43 + 39?

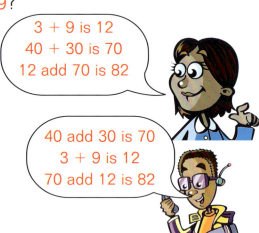

● Have a go

1 Work these out in your head.

a 23 + 48 =   b 54 + 73 =   c 34 + 41 =

d 65 + 29 =   e 35 + 46 =   f 38 + 36 =

2 Complete these addition walls.

```
        65
      32  33
    13  19  14
```

a

b

c

d
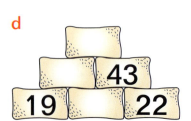

e
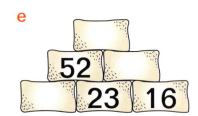

f
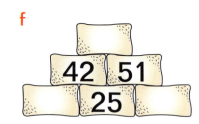

18

Unit 14: Addition patterns

● Remember

Adding numbers that are **multiples** of **10** or **100** are easy if you follow the pattern. Look at these.

6 + 9 = 15   14 + 7 = 21
60 + 90 = 150   140 + 70 = 210
600 + 900 = 1500   140 + 78 = 218

● Have a go

1 Write the answers.

a	b	c	d
8 + 5 = ___	12 + 7 = ___	9 + 16 = ___	13 + 18 = ___
80 + 50 = ___	120 + 70 = ___	90 + 160 = ___	130 + 180 = ___
800 + 500 = ___	1200 + 700 = ___	900 + 1600 = ___	1300 + 1800 = ___
e	f	g	h
18 + 6 = ___	14 + 9 = ___	13 + 8 = ___	15 + 7 = ___
180 + 60 = ___	140 + 90 = ___	130 + 80 = ___	150 + 70 = ___
180 + 63 = ___	140 + 95 = ___	130 + 86 = ___	150 + 79 = ___

2 Use the code to find the name of a special shape.

G	205
S	2050
O	2200
C	270
R	1280
D	2100
A	1580
P	2700
E	2500
N	250

1700 + 400 = _____ ☐
1800 + 700 = _____ ☐
140 + 130 = _____ ☐
1200 + 380 = _____ ☐
160 + 45 = _____ ☐
1300 + 900 = _____ ☐
170 + 80 = _____ ☐

How many sides has the shape got? ____

Unit 15: Finding the difference

● Remember

You find the **difference** between two numbers by counting on.
Count on from the smallest number to the next ten, then on to the largest number.

What is the difference between 38 and 63?
The difference is 25.

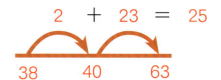

● Have a go

1 Write the difference between these pairs of numbers.
Work them out by counting on in your head.

a 27 and 44 ☐   b 35 and 51 ☐   c 46 and 63 ☐

d 39 and 72 ☐   e 58 and 85 ☐   f 47 and 73 ☐

g 64 and 92 ☐   h 53 and 75 ☐

2 Join the pairs of numbers with a difference of 35.

Unit 16: Mental subtraction

Remember

When you are given a subtraction to work out in your head, there are several different methods you could try.

How would you work out 73 − 38?

73 take away 40 is 33. Add 2 more is 35.

73 take away 30 is 43. 43 take away another 8 is 35.

Counting on from 38 to 40 is 2. 40 to 73 is 33. 33 add 2 is 35.

Have a go

1 Work these out in your head.

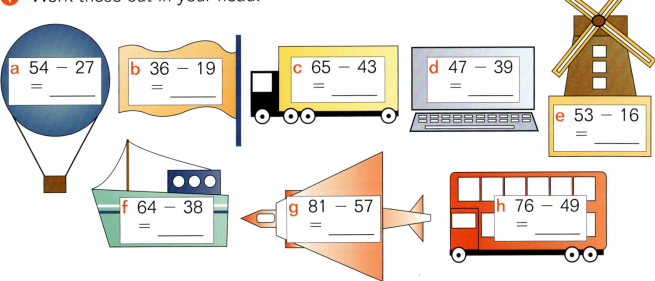

a 54 − 27 = ___
b 36 − 19 = ___
c 65 − 43 = ___
d 47 − 39 = ___
e 53 − 16 = ___
f 64 − 38 = ___
g 81 − 57 = ___
h 76 − 49 = ___

2 Join each sum to its correct answer.

Write a calculation for the extra answer.

53 − 28   15   86 − 41
49 − 34   25   62 − 47
71 − 26   35   77 − 52
64 − 19   45

Unit 17: Using brackets

● Remember

When part of a calculation is in brackets, **you work out the brackets part first**.

(17 − 8) + 4 → 9 + 4 → 13

17 − (8 + 4) → 17 − 12 → 5

● Have a go

1 Answer these.

a (14 − 6) + 5 = ☐
14 − (6 + 5) = ☐

b 17 − (9 − 4) = ☐
(17 − 9) − 4 = ☐

c 15 − (7 − 5) = ☐
(15 − 7) − 5 = ☐

d 18 − (9 + 3) = ☐
(18 − 9) + 3 = ☐

e (19 − 12) + 6 = ☐
19 − (12 + 6) = ☐

2 Draw brackets to make each answer 12.

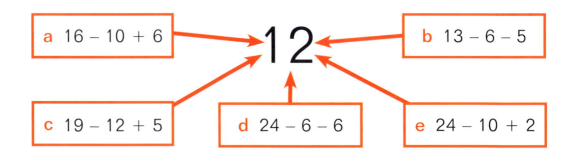

a 16 − 10 + 6
b 13 − 6 − 5
c 19 − 12 + 5
d 24 − 6 − 6
e 24 − 10 + 2

3 Write the missing numbers. Choose from this set of numbers:

3   4   5   6   7

a 15 − (___ + 4) = 5
b (11 − ___) + 7 = 14
c 14 − (8 + ___) = 3
d (12 − ___) − 4 = 1
e (18 + ___) − 8 = 15

Unit 18: Multiplication facts

Remember

Use the **tables facts** you know to help you learn others that you're not sure of.

3 × 5 = 15
3 × 6 is 3 more ⟶ 18

8 × 2 = 16
8 × 4 is double 16 ⟶ 32

10 × 6 = 60
9 × 6 is 6 less ⟶ 54

Remember 3 × 7 is the same as 7 × 3. The answer is the same either way round.

Have a go

1 Use a timer. Answer these as quickly as you can.

a 3 × 7 = ☐   b 4 × 5 = ☐   c 6 × 3 = ☐   d 9 × 2 = ☐

   8 × 10 = ☐   6 × 6 = ☐   9 × 3 = ☐   5 × 7 = ☐

   2 × 8 = ☐   7 × 4 = ☐   8 × 3 = ☐   6 × 7 = ☐

   3 × 3 = ☐   4 × 9 = ☐   5 × 8 = ☐   12 × 2 = ☐

   3 × 11 = ☐   5 × 6 = ☐   10 × 4 = ☐   8 × 4 = ☐

Try it again. Can you beat your best time?

2 Write the missing numbers.

a
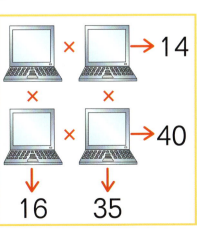

b
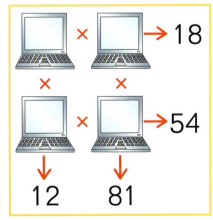

c
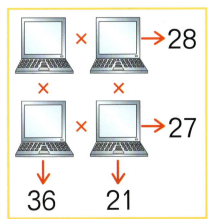

Unit 19: Doubling

🔴 Remember

It is useful to be able to **double** quickly.

Double 160 → double 16 is 32, so double 160 is 320.

Double 4100 → double 41 is 82, so double 4100 is 8200.

Double 74 → double 70 is 140, so double 74 is 148.

🔴 Have a go

1 Use a timer. Answer these as quickly as you can.

a 25 × 2 = _____   49 × 2 = _____   19 × 2 = _____   34 × 2 = _____

b 41 × 2 = _____   27 × 2 = _____   38 × 2 = _____   26 × 2 = _____

c 37 × 2 = _____   46 × 2 = _____   280 × 2 = _____   170 × 2 = _____

d 350 × 2 = _____   420 × 2 = _____   290 × 2 = _____   180 × 2 = _____

e 210 × 2 = _____   480 × 2 = _____   390 × 2 = _____   470 × 2 = _____

Try it again. Can you beat your best time?

2 Write the missing numbers in each table.

a
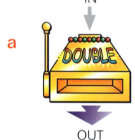

IN	460		180		270	
OUT		900		640		520

b
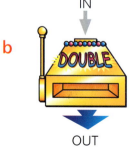

IN	1700		4900		2600	
OUT		7200		4600		9400

24

Unit 20: Mixed calculations

● Remember

Subtraction is the **inverse** of **addition**.
$13 + 8 = 21 \qquad 21 - 8 = 13$

Division is the **inverse** of **multiplication**.
$8 \times 3 = 24 \qquad 24 \div 3 = 8$

You can use this to help work out missing numbers in calculations.

$\boxed{} \div 4 = 5$
$5 \times 4 = 20$
So $20 \div 4 = 5$

● Have a go

1 Write the missing numbers.

a $\boxed{} \div 4 = 5$

b $3 \times \boxed{} = 21$

c $13 + \boxed{} = 24$

d $\boxed{} - 5 = 13$

e $\boxed{} \div 3 = 9$

f $\boxed{} \times 4 = 40$

g $11 + \boxed{} = 29$

h $\boxed{} - 6 = 15$

2 Use the digits 1 to 9.

| 1 | 2 | 3 | 4 | 5 | 6 | 7 | 8 | 9 |

Find a place for each of the digits.

a $\boxed{} \times 4 = 36$

b $1\boxed{} + 6 = 2\boxed{}$

c $\boxed{} \times 5 = 40$

d $\boxed{}\boxed{} \div 5 = 9$

e $18 \div \boxed{} = 3$

f $\boxed{}\boxed{} - 7 = 14$

Unit 21: Division

Remember

If you know your **times tables**, it can help you to divide numbers.
6 × 3 = 18   18 ÷ 3 = 6   18 ÷ 6 = 3
There are several ways of writing a division:

Have a go

1 Use a timer. Answer these as quickly as you can.

a 25 ÷ 5 =   b 16 ÷ 4 =   c 6 ÷ 2 =   d 18 ÷ 3 =

80 ÷ 10 =   24 ÷ 3 =   30 ÷ 5 =   28 ÷ 4 =

50 ÷ 10 =   18 ÷ 2 =   21 ÷ 3 =   24 ÷ 4 =

30 ÷ 10 =   20 ÷ 2 =   45 ÷ 5 =   36 ÷ 2 =

32 ÷ 4 =   15 ÷ 3 =   44 ÷ 11 =   60 ÷ 10 =

Try it again. Can you beat your best time?

2 Use the code to find the names of three planets.

1 Y	2 E	3 T	4 M	5 A
6 R	7 S	8 C	9 U	10 N

a   20 ÷ 5   50 ÷ 10   24 ÷ 4   21 ÷ 3

b   16 ÷ 4   8 ÷ 4   18 ÷ 3   80 ÷ 10   27 ÷ 3   12 ÷ 2   4 ÷ 4

c   28 ÷ 4   15 ÷ 3   12 ÷ 4   90 ÷ 10   36 ÷ 6   40 ÷ 4

Unit 22: Division and remainders

● Remember

If a number cannot be divided exactly, it leaves a **remainder**.

Use your tables facts to help work out the nearest answer below the number, and whatever is left over is the remainder.

43 ÷ 5 = 8 r 3
8 × 5 = 40 ➡ 3 is left over

● Have a go

1 Answer these.

a 49 ÷ 4 = ____ r __   b 32 ÷ 3 = ____ r __   c 51 ÷ 2 = ____ r __

d 41 ÷ 3 = ____ r __   e 58 ÷ 5 = ____ r __   f $\frac{28}{3}$ = ____ r __

g $\frac{63}{2}$ = ____ r __   h $\frac{29}{4}$ = ____ r __   i $\frac{62}{5}$ = ____ r __

j $\frac{74}{3}$ = ____ r __   k 91 ÷ 6 = ____ r __   l 93 ÷ 4 = ____ r __

m 97 ÷ 4 = ____ r __   n 86 ÷ 3 = ____ r __   o 88 ÷ 6 = ____ r __

2 Match each division to a remainder. Write a division for the spare remainder.

Remainder

50 ÷ 4

63 ÷ 6

87 ÷ 8

89 ÷ 10

74 ÷ 5

80 ÷ 9

37 ÷ 3

54 ÷ 7

____ ÷ ____

Unit 23: Money

● Remember

There are **100 pence** in **£1**.
When you write amounts as pounds and pence, you separate the pounds from the pence with a **decimal point**.

£1.80 = 180p
£2.05 = 205p
£4.29 = 429p
£0.75 = 75p

● Have a go

1 Convert these to pence.

a £2.50 = _____ p   b £3.05 = _____ p   c £1.85 = _____ p

d £2.63 = _____ p   e £0.92 = _____ p   f £3.17 = _____ p

2 Convert these to pounds and pence.

a 370p = £ _____   b 205p = £ _____   c 565p = £ _____

d 109p = £ _____   e 342p = £ _____   f 87p = £ _____

3 Look at the menu.

Which coins would you need to buy each item?

a Filled roll _____

b Sandwich _____

c Soup _____

d Sausage roll _____

e Toastie _____

MENU

Filled roll £1.05
Sandwich £1.19
Soup £1.89
Sausage roll £0.87
Toastie £2.15

Unit 24: Money calculations

Remember

When you **add** amounts in your head, it is sometimes easier to add the pounds and then the pence: £4.70 + £3.40 ➡ £7 add 110p ➡ £8.10.
When you **subtract** amounts or find differences in your head, it is sometimes easier to count on: £9.30 – £6.90 ➡ £6.90 up to £7 is 10p. £7 up to £9.30 is £2.30. £2.30 add 10p is £2.40.

Have a go

1 Total these amounts.

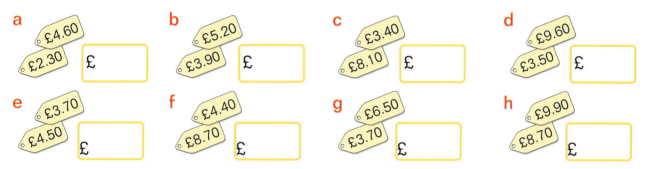

a £4.60, £2.30 £
b £5.20, £3.90 £
c £3.40, £8.10 £
d £9.60, £3.50 £
e £3.70, £4.50 £
f £4.40, £8.70 £
g £6.50, £3.70 £
h £9.90, £8.70 £

2 What is the difference between these pairs of prices?

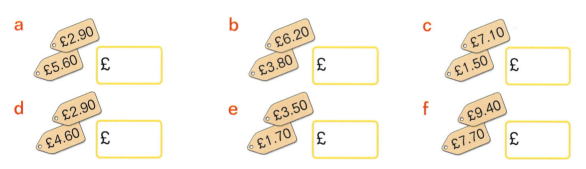

a £2.90, £5.60 £
b £6.20, £3.80 £
c £7.10, £1.50 £
d £2.90, £4.60 £
e £3.50, £1.70 £
f £9.40, £7.70 £

3 Here are some entrance tickets for different attractions.

Theme Park Admit one: £9.20
THEATRE Matinée Performance Stalls: £7.90
LEISURE CENTRE Swimming – open session Adult Member: £2.70
SAFARI PARK Day Pass: £8.50

a What is the total cost of visiting the Theme Park, Safari Park and Leisure Centre? _____

b What change from £20 will there be for tickets for the Theatre and the Safari Park? _____

c Which two attractions, when totalled, would give change of £2.90 from £20? _____

29

Unit 25: Mixed problems

● Remember

Word problems need careful preparation.

Example: What is the change from £5 for two magazines costing £2.20 each?
• Read the problem and work out the calculations you need.
£2.20 × 2 = £4.40
£5.00 − £4.40 = 60p
• After the calculation check that you've answered the problem correctly. What is the question actually asking?

● Have a go

1 Answer these word problems.

a There are thirty marbles in Joe's bag and eighteen in Donna's bag. How many more marbles has Joe than Donna? _____

b In a box of chocolates there are two rows of sixteen chocolates. If seven have been eaten altogether, how many chocolates are left? _____

c Sam has sixty stickers. He keeps fifteen and shares the rest equally between five friends. How many does each friend get? _____

d Two plums weigh 80 g each. If an apple weighs the same as two plums, what is the weight of an apple? _____

e Josh has forty sweets. He gives half of his sweets to Ben and half of what is left to Alice. How many sweets does he still have? _____

f Forty-seven people are going on a trip. Minibuses can take ten people. How many minibuses will be needed? _____

2 Answer these puzzles.

a I think of a number and then divide it by 5. The answer is 8. What was my number? _____

b I think of a number and then multiply it by 3. The answer is 18. What was my number? _____

c I think of a number and then divide it by 4. The answer is 4 less than 10. What was my number? _____

d I think of a number and then add 15. The answer is 40. What was my number? _____

e I think of a number and then subtract 9. The answer is 7. What was my number? _____

Unit 26: Mixed puzzles

● Remember

Maths puzzles can sometimes be quite tricky. Prepare for these by making a small set of 1–9 number cards from paper or thin card.

● Have a go

1 Arrange the numbers from 1 to 9 in the circles so that each side of the square adds up to 12.

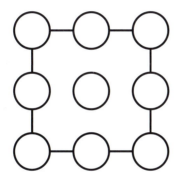

2 Use each of the numbers from 1 to 9. Write three numbers in each star so that the total in each is 15. Find different ways to do it.

3 Use each of the digits 3 to 8 once only to complete these.

a 3☐ + ☐3 = 91

b 8☐ − 49 = ☐7

c ☐7 × 2 = 94

d 2☐ ÷ 3 = 9

31

Unit 27: 2D shapes

Remember

A **polygon** is any 2D shape with straight sides. Look at the number of sides to help you recognise different polygons.

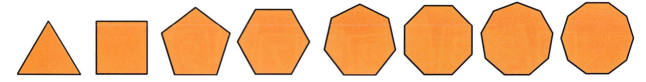

The sides and angles of a **regular polygon** are all equal.

Have a go

1 Name each shape. Tick the regular polygons.

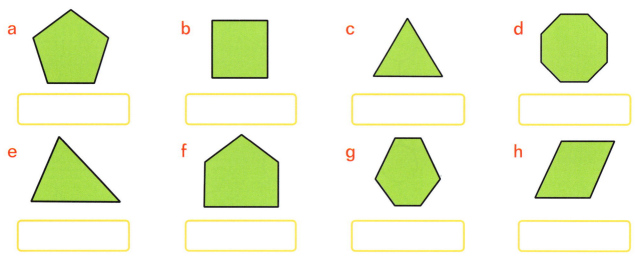

2 Tick the odd one out in each set.

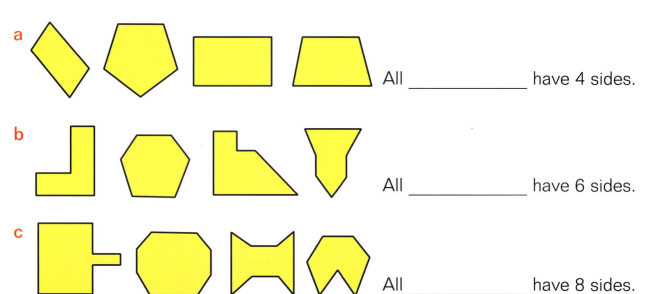

a All _____ have 4 sides.

b All _____ have 6 sides.

c All _____ have 8 sides.

Unit 28: Symmetry

● Remember

Shapes are **symmetrical** if they are the same either side of a **mirror line**, like a reflection.

The sides and angles of a **regular polygon** are all equal and they have lines of symmetry.

line of symmetry

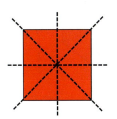

● Have a go

① Draw the reflection of each of these.

a 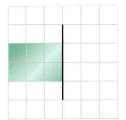   b 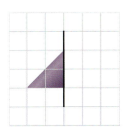   c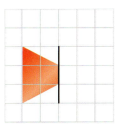

d 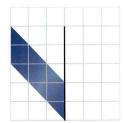   e 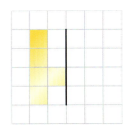   f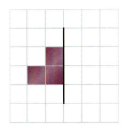

② Draw the lines of symmetry on each of these regular shapes.

a   b   c

____ lines of symmetry   ____ lines of symmetry   ____ lines of symmetry

d   e

____ lines of symmetry   ____ lines of symmetry

f What do you notice about the lines of symmetry of regular shapes?

_____

33

Unit 29: Naming 3D solids

Remember

These shapes are all **3D solids**. Each side is called a **face**.

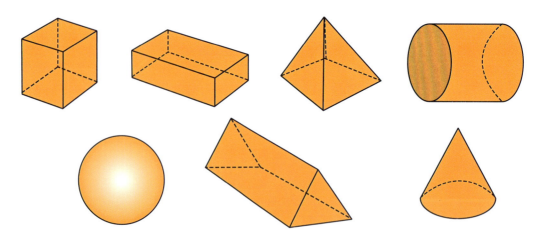

Have a go

1 Join each solid to its name.

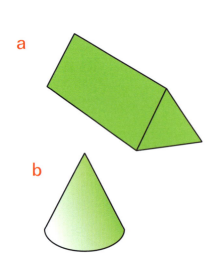

prism

cuboid

pyramid

cone

cylinder

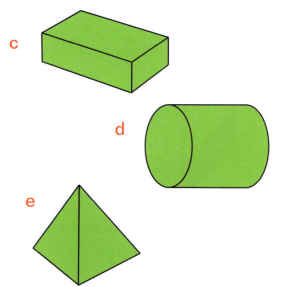

2 Name these shapes.

a I have four triangle faces. What am I? _____

b I have two square faces and four rectangle faces. What am I? _____

c I have six square faces. What am I? _____

d I am completely curved. What am I? _____

Unit 30: Properties of 3D solids

Remember

3D solids are solid shapes with three dimensions:

width, depth and height.

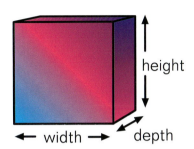

Have a go

1. Tick the odd solid out in each set.

a

b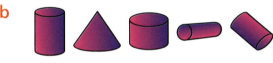

c

d

e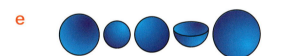

2. Write the numbers of faces on each of these solids.

a

____ square face and
____ triangle faces

b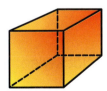

____ square faces and
____ rectangle faces

c

____ triangle faces and
____ rectangle faces

d

____ triangle faces

35

Unit 31: Angles

● Remember

Angles are measured in degrees (°).
- A complete turn is 360°.
- Half a turn is 180°.
- A quarter turn is 90°, also called a right angle.
- Half a right angle is 45°.

Here are eight compass directions: North, North-east, East, South-east, South, South-west, West, North-west.

This direction is clockwise:

This direction is anticlockwise:

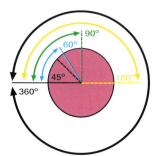

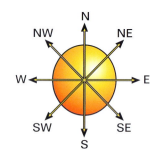

● Have a go

1 Estimate each of these angles.

a  ___°

b  ___°

c ___°

2 Write which compass point you will face after each turn.

a Face North to start each time.

Make a 90° turn clockwise. ____

Make a 180° turn anticlockwise. ____

Make a 45° turn clockwise. ____

b Face South to start each time.

Make a 180° turn anticlockwise. ____

Make a 45° turn anticlockwise. ____

Make a 90° turn clockwise. ____

c Face East to start each time.

Make a 360° turn clockwise. ____

Make a 90° turn clockwise. ____

Make a 45° turn anticlockwise. ____

d Face West to start each time.

Make a 90° turn anticlockwise. ____

Make a 45° turn clockwise. ____

Make a 180° turn clockwise. ____

Unit 32: Coordinates

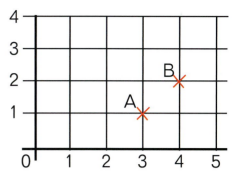

Remember

A **coordinate** is a position on a **grid**.
The coordinates of A are (3, 1)
Read the **horizontal** coordinate first
and then the **vertical** coordinate.

A **translation** is a slide left, right, up or down.
The cross at A has translated 1 square right and 1 square up. The new position B is (4, 2).

Have a go

1. Look at these coordinates and then answer the questions.

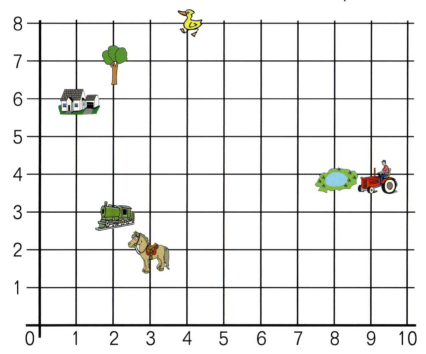

a What is at position:
(1, 6) _____   (8, 4) _____   (3, 2) _____   (2, 7) _____

b What are the coordinates for:
the duck (____)   the train (____)   the tractor (____)   the house (____)

c Draw each object on the grid to show the translations. Write the new coordinates.

Tree ⟶ translate 2 squares right and 3 squares down.   (___) (___)

House ⟶ translate 4 squares right and 1 square up.   (___) (___)

Pond ⟶ translate 1 square left and 4 squares down.   (___) (___)

37

Unit 33: Measuring length

Remember

Long distances can be measured in **kilometres** and **metres**.

1 kilometre (km) = 1000 metres (m)
1 metre (m) = 100 centimetres (cm)

Have a go

1 Write these lengths.

a 3000 m = _____ km

b 9000 m = _____ km

c 8 km = _____ m

d 1000 cm = _____ m

e 400 cm = _____ m

f 7 m = _____ cm

g 15 m = _____ cm

h 11 km = _____ m

2 A balloon race starts from Ashford. Each balloon lands at a village. Write the distances in kilometres and the village each balloon landed at.

a Mighty Mo: 6000 m ⟶ _____ km. Landed at _____

b Fab Flyer: 12 000 m ⟶ _____ km. Landed at _____

c Super Star: 20 000 m ⟶ _____ km. Landed at _____

d Speed Dragon: 10 000 m ⟶ _____ km. Landed at _____

e Top Dog: 18 000 m ⟶ _____ km. Landed at _____

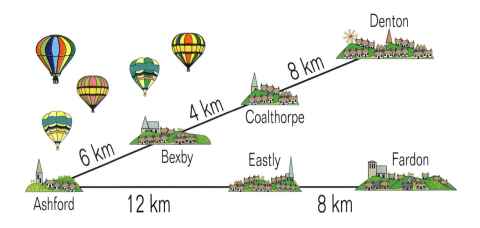

Unit 34: Measuring mass

Remember

You measure the **weight** or **mass** of an object using **kilograms** (kg) and **grams** (g).

1000 g → 1 kg
750 g → $\frac{3}{4}$ kg
500 g → $\frac{1}{2}$ kg
250 g → $\frac{1}{4}$ kg
100 g → $\frac{1}{10}$ kg

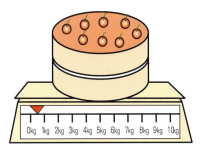

Find something that weighs about $\frac{1}{2}$ kg and check it on some scales.

Have a go

1 Write the missing amounts

a 3000 g = _____ kg
b 2250 g = _____ kg
c 5500 g = _____ kg
d 3100 g = _____ kg
e _____ g = 1 kg
f _____ g = $3\frac{1}{2}$ kg
g _____ g = 10 kg
h _____ g = $2\frac{1}{10}$ kg

2 Write each weight to the nearest half unit on the scale.

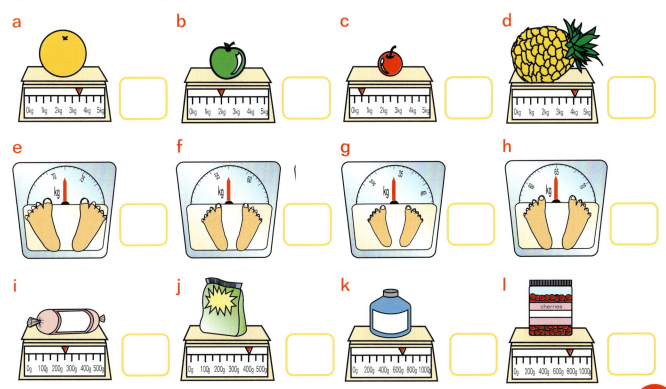

39

Unit 35: Measuring capacity

● Remember

You measure **capacity** using **litres (l)** and **millilitres (ml)**.

1000 ml = 1 l   750 ml = $\frac{3}{4}$ l   500 ml = $\frac{1}{2}$ l

250 ml = $\frac{1}{4}$ l   100 ml = $\frac{1}{10}$ l

Find different jugs and containers. What is the capacity of each of them?

● Have a go

1 Write the missing amounts.

a 4000 ml = _____ l   b _____ ml = $2\frac{1}{2}$ l   c 1500 ml = _____ l

d _____ ml = $1\frac{3}{4}$ l   e 5250 ml = _____ l   f _____ ml = 10 l

g 2100 ml = _____ l   h _____ ml = $4\frac{1}{10}$ l

2 Write the capacity each shows.

a  ml

b ml

c 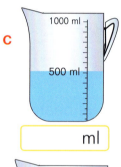 ml

d 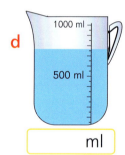 ml

e l

f l

g 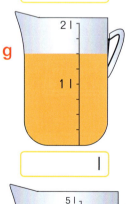 l

h 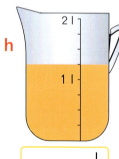 l

i 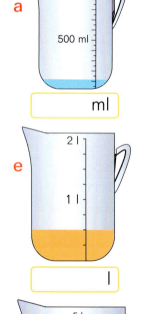 l

j 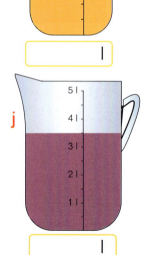 l

k 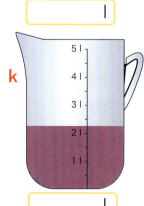 l

l  l

40

Unit 36: Perimeter

● Remember

The **perimeter** of a shape is the distance all around the edge.

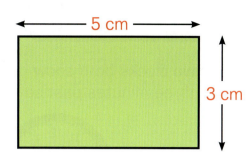

The perimeter of this shape is 5 cm + 5 cm + 3 cm + 3 cm = 16 cm.

● Have a go

1 What is the perimeter of each of these rectangles?

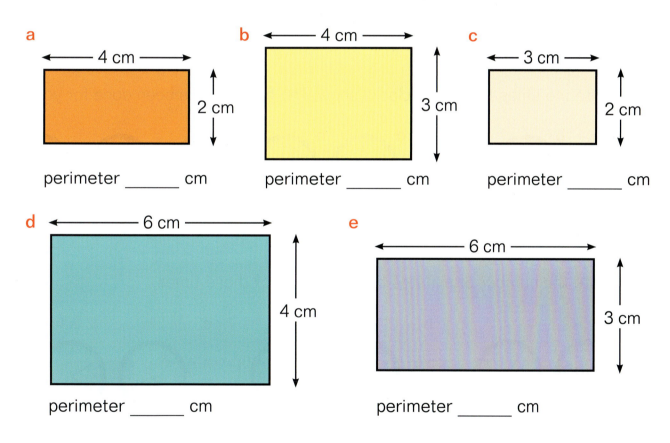

2 Measure the perimeter of each of these shapes.

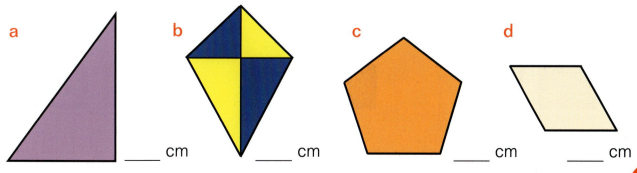

Unit 37: Time

● Remember

These two clocks both show twenty-three minutes past seven.

These two clocks both show forty-eight minutes past seven.

There are **60 minutes in an hour**, so 7:48 is 48 minutes past the hour. Notice that the hour hand moves towards the next hour.

● Have a go

1 Write the times that these clocks show. The first one has been done for you.

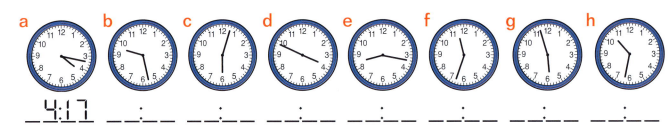

a 4:17   b __:__   c __:__   d __:__   e __:__   f __:__   g __:__   h __:__

2 Write the number of minutes between each of these times.

a

_____ minutes

b

_____ minutes

c

_____ minutes

d

_____ minutes

e

_____ minutes

f

_____ minutes

Unit 38: Calendars

Remember

This is a good way to learn how many **days** there are in each **month**.

Put your hands together and look at your knuckles.
January is on the first knuckle of your left hand.
All the 'knuckle months' have 31 days.
February has 28 days.
The other four months have 30 days.

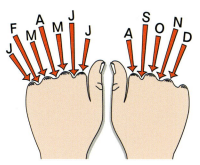

Have a go

1 Use the calendar to answer these questions.

a Which months end on a Friday?

_____

b Which months start on a Saturday?

_____

c How many days are there in October? ____

d How many Sundays are there in May? ____

2 Use the calendar to answer these problems.

a A Nature Club meets on the first Thursday of each month. Write the dates of all the meetings.

____ Jan   ____ Feb   ____ Mar   ____ Apr   ____ May   ____ June

____ July   ____ Aug   ____ Sep   ____ Oct   ____ Nov   ____ Dec

b The club members cleaned a village pond. They started on 6th June and finished on 20th July.
How many weekends did they work? _____

c The club goes on a summer camp for a week beginning on the first Friday in August. What dates do they leave and return?

Leave _____   Return _____

43

Unit 39: Pictograms

Remember

Pictograms use pictures to show amounts.
Look carefully to check what each single picture represents.
This pictogram shows the number of birds visiting a bird table.

represents 5 birds

represents less than 5 birds

Can you work out how many birds came to the bird table between 1.00 p.m. and 2.00 p.m.?

Have a go

represents 2 animals

represents 1 animal

1 These are the number of different animals treated by a vet in a week.
Use the diagram to answer these questions.

a How many animals were seen on Thursday? _____
b Which day had the most number of visits? _____
c On which day were 13 animals treated by the vet? _____
d On which two days were the same number of animals treated? _____
e How many animals were seen altogether? _____

2 The diagram below shows the types of different animals seen by the vet in a month. All the answers will be approximate.

a How many birds were seen by the vet? Between _____ and _____.
b How many small pets were seen by the vet? Between _____ and _____.
c How many more dogs than cats were seen? _____

represents 10 animals

represents less than 10 animals

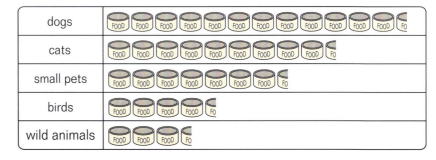

44

Unit 40: Bar charts

Remember

A **bar chart** shows information as a graph. Read the scale and labels on the **axes** carefully.

How many hours of sunshine were there on Wednesday?

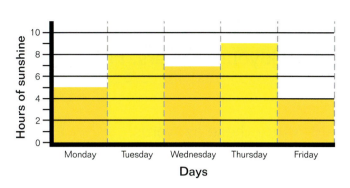

Have a go

1 These are the temperatures in Rome and London for a week in March. Use the graphs to answer the questions below.

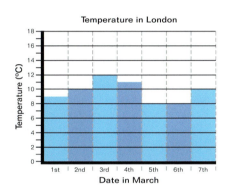
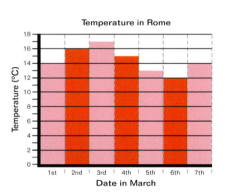

London:	Rome:
a Which date had the highest temperature? _____	a What was the temperature on the 5th March? _____
b What temperature was reached on the 4th March? _____	b On which date did the temperature reach 17 °C? _____
c Which two dates had the same lowest temperature? _____ and _____	c Which date had the lowest temperature? _____
d What was the difference in temperature between the 1st and 3rd March? _____	d What was the difference in temperature between the 4th and 6th March? _____

2 Compare the two graphs.

a How much hotter was Rome than London on the 1st March? _____
b On which date was Rome 6 °C hotter than London? _____
c What was the difference in temperature between the hottest days in London and Rome? _____
d On which day in Rome was the temperature the same as the hottest day in London? _____

Test 1

Check how much you have learned.

Answer the questions.
Mark your answers. Fill in your scores.

SCORE

1 Write these as words:

a 4673 → _____

b 2004 → _____

c 3096 → _____

out of 3

2 Write the missing numbers.

75   71   [ ]   [ ]   59   55   [ ]

out of 3

3 Write the lengths.

a 7000 m = [ ] km   b 11 km = [ ] m

c 300 cm = [ ] m   d 8 m = [ ] cm

out of 4

4 This pictogram shows the number of people buying from an ice-cream van for five days.
On which day did 75 people buy ice creams?

_____

 represents 10 people

represents 5 people

Monday	
Tuesday	
Wednesday	
Thursday	
Friday	
Saturday	
Sunday	

out of 1

5 Write the missing numbers.

out of 3

a 9 + [ ] = 17   b [ ] − 6 = 8   c 7 + [ ] = 13

46

6 What fraction of these cakes have cherries?

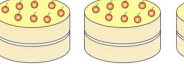

out of 1

7 Join the names to the correct shapes.

hexagon

pentagon

quadrilateral

heptagon

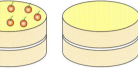

a

b

c d

out of 4

8 Use the calendar below to answer these.

a What is the date of the second Saturday in March? ____

b On which day is the 1st April? _____

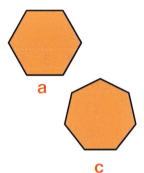

March					
M		3	10	17	24	31
T		4	11	18	25
W		5	12	19	26
T		6	13	20	27
F		7	14	21	28
S	1	8	15	22	29
S	2	9	16	23	30

out of 2

out of 2

9 Work these out in your head.

a 37 + 54 = ☐   b 46 + 28 = ☐

out of 1

10 What is the difference between 38 and 72? ☐

Total out of 24

47

Test 2

Check how much you have learned.

Answer the questions.
Mark your answers. Fill in your scores.

SCORE

① Write the missing numbers in this chain.

4105 → + 100 → ☐ → − 1000 → ☐ → + 10 → ☐

out of 3

② Shade in the numbers following these rules:

Start at one and count on in threes.

Circle the number that would **not** be in your sequence

34   36   40

1	2	3	4	5
6	7	8	9	10
11	12	13	14	15
16	17	18	19	20
21	22	23	24	25

out of 1

③ What is the perimeter of this rectangle? _____

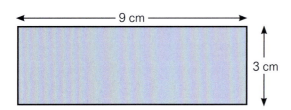

out of 1

④ This graph shows the flavours of sweets in a giant box of fruit chews.

How many more lemon sweets than orange sweets were in the box? _____

out of 1

48

5 Write the missing numbers for this machine.

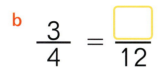

IN	19		23		25	
OUT		4		9		18

out of 6

6 Complete these equivalent fractions.

a $\dfrac{1}{4} = \dfrac{\square}{12}$

b $\dfrac{3}{4} = \dfrac{\square}{12}$

out of 2

7 Draw the reflection of this shape.

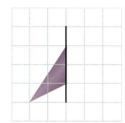

out of 1

8 Write the times these clocks show.

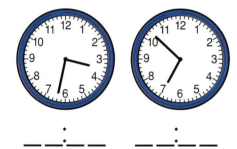

__ __ : __ __   __ __ : __ __

out of 2

9 Write the answers.

a 70 + 90 = ____

b 700 + 900 = ____

c 160 + 80 = ____

d 160 + 84 = ____

out of 4

10 Work these out mentally.

a 53 − 29 = ____

b 76 − 47 = ____

out of 2

Total out of 23

49

Test 3

Check how much you have learned.

Answer the questions.
Mark your answers. Fill in your scores.

SCORE

1 Answer these.

a What is the next even number after 378? _____

b What is the next odd number after 799? _____

out of 2

2 What is the weight of this cake?

Write the answer in kilograms and grams.

____ kg = ____ g

out of 2

3 Answer these.

a 6 × 5 = ☐   b 7 × 3 = ☐   c 4 × 4 = ☐

out of 3

4 Write the missing numbers.

a 17 + ☐ = 30   b ☐ ÷ 3 = 6

c 10 × ☐ = 80   d ☐ − 8 = 14

out of 4

5 Join the names to the correct solids.

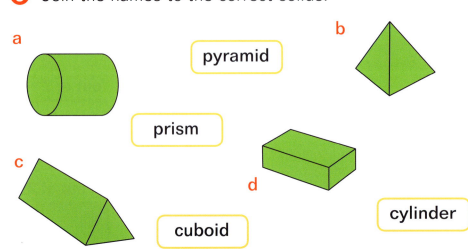

out of 4

50

7 a What are the coordinates of A and B?

A ⟶ _____

B ⟶ _____

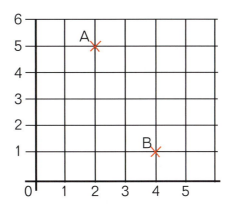

 out of 3

b A and B are two corners of a triangle.
The third corner of a triangle (C) is at (5, 4). Mark the point and draw the triangle.

8 Write these numbers in order starting with the smallest.

6095   6900   609   6509   695

_____ _____ _____ _____ _____

 out of 1

Answer these.

 out of 3

a 24 ÷ 4 = ☐   b 45 ÷ 5 = ☐   c 27 ÷ 3 = ☐

9 Write the total as pence and pounds.

_____ p = £ _____

 out of 2

10 Answer this.

Ryan bought two t-shirts, each costing £3.40.

How much change did he have from £10? _____

 out of 1

Total out of 25

51

Test 4

Check how much you have learned.

Answer the questions.
Mark your answers. Fill in your scores.

SCORE

① Circle the multiples of 2.
Tick the multiples of 5.

28   35   70   87   100   96   85

out of 2

② What amount is shown in the jug?
Write the answer in litres and millilitres.

_____ l = _____ ml

out of 2

③ Write the missing numbers in this table.

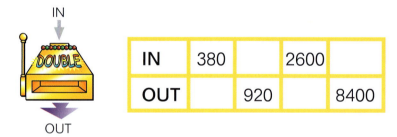

IN	380		2600	
OUT		920		8400

out of 4

④ Answer these.

a (19 – 7) + 6 = _____   b 19 – (7 + 6) = _____

out of 2

⑤ Sketch and name the 3D solid this is describing:

This solid has two triangle faces and three rectangle faces.

Its name is a _____.

out of 2

6 I am facing North. If I turn clockwise 180° and then 45° anticlockwise, in which direction am I now facing?

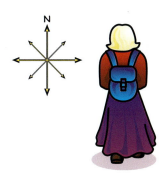

I am now facing _____

out of 1

7 Write the signs < or > for this.

2813 ___ 2193 ___ 2139

out of 1

8 Answer these.

a 59 ÷ 4 = _____ r ___

b 87 ÷ 5 = _____ r ___

c 68 ÷ 3 = _____ r ___

out of 3

9 Answer these.

a What is the total cost of stamps for the two parcels?
_____

b What is the difference in the cost of the stamps?
_____

out of 2

10 Use the digits 1–6 to complete these.

a ☐5 + 28 = 7☐

b ☐6 − 3☐ = 25

c 3☐ × ☐ = 72

out of 6

Total out of 25

53

Parents' notes

Unit 1: Place value   The place value is the position or place of a digit in a number. The same digit has a different value at different places in a number. Your child needs to know the value of the thousands, hundreds, tens and ones digits in a four-digit number. It is a common mistake to muddle up the digits when reading numbers. Let your child practise counting in 1000s, 100s and 10s to get used to the value of different numbers.

Unit 2: Digits   Your child should know the value of the thousands, hundreds, tens and ones in a four-digit number and know how digits are changed by adding and subtracting from these numbers.

Unit 3: Sequences   Number sequences are lists of numbers with a pattern between each number. Encourage your child to work out the difference between each number, as that gives the clue to the missing numbers.

Unit 4: Patterns on grids   Number sequences are lists of numbers with a pattern between each number. They are shown here in grids rather than lines, but the same rules apply. Sequences are different from multiples because they can begin at any number. Multiples are special sequences.

Unit 5: Comparing numbers   The symbols for 'more than' ($>$) and 'less than' ($<$) can cause confusion. A simple rule is that the signs, which look like arrow heads, always point to the smaller number: $481 > 427$ and $375 < 394$.

Unit 6: Ordering numbers   Place value is the position or place of a digit in a number. The same digit has a different value at different places in a number. Encourage your child to see four-digit numbers as thousands, hundreds, tens and ones. So, 4852 needs to be seen as $4000 + 800 + 50 + 2$. When numbers are put in order of size, make sure that your child looks at each of the digits starting with the thousands down to the ones.

Unit 7: Odd and even numbers   Your child needs to recognise odd and even numbers up to 1000 and beyond. Make sure that your child knows that it is the 'ones' digit that shows whether a number is odd or even. An even number can be divided equally by 2, whereas odd numbers leave a remainder of 1 when divided by 2.

Unit 8: Multiples   Your child needs to recognise multiples of 2, 5 and 10. Make sure that he or she understands that multiples don't stop at $10\times$ a number, but go on and on. The important thing is to begin to recognise the 'rule' for a set of multiples. For example, we know that 125 is a multiple of 5 because the last digit is a 5.

Unit 9: Fractions   Check that your child knows that the number above the line of a fraction is the numerator and the number below the line is the denominator. If your child needs to colour, for example, $\frac{3}{5}$ of a shape, make sure he or she understands that it is necessary to cut it into five equal parts (shown by the denominator) and then shade three of these parts (shown by the numerator). Check that your child just changes the numerator when adding and subtracting fractions with the same denominator – the denominator does not change.

Unit 10: Equivalent fractions   Check that your child knows that the number above the line of a fraction is the numerator and the number below the line is the denominator. Make sure that your child understands that $\frac{1}{2}$ and $\frac{2}{4}$ are the same by getting him or her to colour in two identical shapes that are divided into four equal parts.

Unit 11: Addition and subtraction facts   The three numbers that make up an addition or subtraction fact are a 'trio'. So 5, 12 and 7 are a trio: $5 + 7 = 12$,

$7 + 5 = 12$, $12 - 7 = 5$, $12 - 5 = 7$. With missing number problems it is often best to use the numbers that are given out of the 'trio' to help work out the missing number.

Unit 12: Function machines Addition and subtraction are inverse operations – in other words, they are opposite to each other. This is important to understand, as missing numbers in calculations can be worked out by looking at the facts given and using the inverse operation.

Unit 13: Mental addition Most of the mental addition methods that children use involve 'partitioning', or breaking numbers up to make each part easier to add. There is no set standard method, so try to encourage your child to look at the numbers to be added and choose the most appropriate strategy. This could be by adding the tens first, or starting with the ones, or rounding the numbers to the nearest ten.

Unit 14: Addition patterns Your child should be able to recognise the pattern in adding multiples of 10 and 100. Point out the connection between the number of zeros in the numbers added and the number of zeros in the answer. Whether you add units or tens, the digits are the same – it is their place value that changes.

Unit 15: Finding the difference There are many different strategies for subtraction, including counting on and counting back. If you need to find the difference between two numbers, counting on from the smaller number to the next ten and then on to the larger number is a useful strategy. Your child may find it helpful to picture a number line in his or her head.

Unit 16: Mental subtraction Encourage your child to try out the different methods for mental subtraction that are shown, such as counting on and counting back.

Unit 17: Using brackets Brackets in a calculation show that the part of the calculation in the brackets needs to be worked out first. To begin with, your child may need to write the answer to the part in the brackets above the calculation so that the rest of it can be worked out. With the missing numbers problems, your child may need to use trial-and-improvement methods, putting numbers in to see if they work and then changing them for the correct answer.

Unit 18: Multiplication facts Your child needs to try to learn all the multiplication tables facts up to 10×10. He or she should practise the facts and write down the ones that cause problems. Use the facts that your child knows to work out the others. For example, if your child knows that $5 \times 8 = 40$, then 6×8 is just 8 more. It is important that your child knows that, for example, 7×3 and 3×7 give the same answer.

Unit 19: Doubling Encourage your child to break the numbers down as shown in the examples. Your child needs to understand the relationship between the tens and the units, for example, double 13 is 26, so double 130 is 260. Practice will help your child to recognise the patterns of doubling more quickly.

Unit 20: Mixed calculations Addition and subtraction are inverse operations – in other words, they are opposite to each other. Multiplication and division are also inverse operations. This is important to understand, as missing numbers in calculations can be worked out by looking at the facts given and using the inverse operation.

Unit 21: Division Division facts are easy to work out if your child knows the times tables. A question such as $28 \div 4$ can be seen as 'how many 4s in 28?' If they know that seven 4s are 28, then the division can be quickly worked out.

Unit 22: Division and remainders   It is important for your child to understand that division does not always produce an exact answer – there can be a remainder left over. Tables facts can be used to work out the nearest answer below the number, and whatever is left over is the remainder. For example, $32 \div 5 = 6$ r 2; $6 \times 5 = 30$, 2 is left over.

Unit 23: Money   Your child needs to handle money amounts over £1 and relate the amounts to written prices. Make sure that he or she understands that, for example, 245p is £2.45. With money, the decimal point is used primarily as a separator, to separate the pounds from the pence.

Unit 24: Money calculations   Your child needs to handle money amounts over £1 and relate amounts to written prices. Make sure that he or she understands that, for example, 245p is £2.45. When adding money amounts in your head, it can help to add the pounds first, then the pennies and put them together. When subtracting or working out change, it can help to count on from the lower amount.

Unit 25: Mixed problems   With word problems, encourage your child to read the problem carefully and try to picture the problem as a scene in his or her head. Your child should then work out what sort of calculation is needed before answering it. Once your child has an answer, he or she needs to look back at the problem to see exactly what it was asking for as an answer.

Unit 26: Mixed puzzles   Encourage your child to play around with the number cards 1–9 to work out the problems. For the calculations, your child may have to try several numbers and check the answers before finding which numbers are correct.

Unit 27: 2D shapes   Polygons are two-dimensional shapes with straight sides. Each has a special name related to the number of sides, so any shape with four straight sides is a quadrilateral. Then, within that set there are further names for shapes with certain features. Make sure that your child recognises that some shapes may have more than one name. For example, a square is a special rectangle and also a type of quadrilateral.

Unit 28: Symmetry   For many children the idea of symmetry is not a difficult one. When they are building, they often naturally make their model symmetrical. To confirm ideas of symmetry allow your child to fold a small piece of paper in half (newspaper will do) and cut a shape out of the fold. When the shape is opened out it will have a line of symmetry – the fold line. As a further step, fold the paper two or three times before cutting out to create a shape with more than one line of symmetry.

Unit 29: Naming 3D solids   Point out solids around the house and outside that are shaped like a cube, cuboid, sphere, cone, prism, pyramid and cylinder. Ask your child to describe each solid and point out the faces, describing the shapes of the faces and the number of faces that a solid has.

Unit 30: Properties of 3D solids   Look at 3D shapes that you have in your house, such as a television or football. Ask your child to point out the width of the object or the height.

Unit 31: Angles   Your child needs to know the eight main points of the compass. He or she also needs to know that there are 360° in a complete turn, 90° in a quarter turn or right angle, and so on. Practise with your child facing in a certain direction, saying which compass point it is and then turning clockwise or anticlockwise to specified angles or other compass points. Your child should begin to get a feel for the size of different angles and how they relate to the main compass directions.

Unit 32: Coordinates   A common error when reading coordinates is to get the two numbers the wrong way around. In the example, position (4, 2) is shown as B. Encourage your child to start at zero and go across the horizontal x-axis until level with the B (across 4) and then up to B (up 2). This will get your child into the habit of reading across the x-axis before going up the y-axis.

Unit 33: Measuring length   To help your child get an idea of approximate lengths of longer distances, find places that are approximately 100 m, 200 m, 500 m and 1 km from your home. Use these to help your child estimate other distances.

Unit 34: Measuring mass   Mass and weight are different from each other. Mass is the amount of matter an object contains. Weight is the heaviness of an object or person; gravity pulls objects down and gives them weight. However, they both use kilograms and grams as units of measure. At this level, we mainly refer to weight only.

Unit 35: Measuring capacity   Your child needs to know that a litre is equal to 1000 millilitres, half a litre is equal to 500 millilitres, and so on. Talk with your child about which liquids are measured in millilitres and which in litres. Look for examples of them on food labels.

Unit 36: Perimeter   Your child needs to understand that the perimeter of a shape is the distance all around the edge, so he or she needs to add up all the sides. Any shape can have a perimeter, not just a rectangle or square. Your child could practise measuring and calculating the perimeter of various shapes, such as a book or the top of a table.

Unit 37: Time   It is important that your child can tell the time from digital clocks and clocks with hands. Remember that there are two ways of saying the time after the half hour. For example, 2.50 can be said as *Two fifty* or *Ten to three*. The 'minutes to' way of saying the time is oral, not written. The 'minutes past' way is how it is written in timetables and listings, and is the same as digital time. Remind your child that there are 60 minutes in an hour. When calculating how many minutes between two times, it may help your child to imagine a time line, or to work in stages – count on to the next five minutes, half hour or hour.

Unit 38: Calendars   Your child needs to know the names and order of the months in the year, as well as how many days are in each month. Use the knuckle method to help your child learn the number of days and make sure that a calendar is used regularly.

Unit 39: Pictograms   Pictograms are a very popular way of showing information as a graph. Make sure that your child understands that, for these pictograms, each picture represents two, five or ten items. If a whole picture represents ten items, then half a picture can represent between one and nine items, so an exact number can't be given. It is important to read all the information about each pictogram to get a good understanding of it.

Unit 40: Bar charts   Bar charts or bar graphs are a very clear way of showing information as a graph. They can be horizontal or vertical in layout. Make sure that your child understands that the scale on each of these graphs is labelled in twos. It is important to read all the information about each graph, such as title and axis headings, so that your child has a good understanding of the graph.

Answers

Unit 1: Place value (page 6)

1
- a 60
- b 2000   5
- c 700   10   4
- d 3000   900   7
- e 1000   200   30
- f 2000   800   20   1
- g 3000   200   80   5
- h 9000   300   70   6

2

Across	Down
1. 6193	1. 6804
3. 3208	2. 9400
4. 1794	4. 1043
6. 3923	5. 9352

Unit 2: Digits (page 7)

1
- a 1896   1897   1898   1899
- b 6047   6046   6045   6044
- c 3194   3204   3214   3224
- d 2643   2633   2623   2613

2
- a 3759   3859   3959   4059
- b 5178   5078   4978   4878
- c 3093   4093   5093   6093
- d 6928   5928   4928   3928

Unit 3: Sequences (page 8)

1
- a Rule +5   38   43   48   53
- b Rule −2   33   31   29   27
- c Rule +3   66   69   72   75
- d Rule +4   54   58   62   66
- e Rule −10   54   44   34   24
- f Rule −5   67   62   57   52

2
- a 250   400
- b 425   350   325
- c 1010   810   510
- d 225   275   300

Unit 4: Patterns on grids (page 9)

1
- a numbers shaded: 2, 5, 8, 11, 14, 17, 20, 23
  number circled: 35
- b numbers shaded: 2, 6, 10, 14, 18, 22
  number circled: 38

- c numbers shaded: 3, 7, 11, 15, 19, 23, 27, 31, 35
  number circled: 43
- d numbers shaded: 1, 4, 7, 10, 13, 16, 19, 22, 25, 28, 31, 34
  number circled: 40

2 Ask your child to describe the patterns.

Unit 5: Comparing numbers (page 10)

1
- a < b < c > d > e >
- f < g > h > i <

2
- a > < b < < c < >
- d > < e < > f > >

3
- a 2947   2948   2949   2950   2951
- b 4810   4809   4808

Unit 6: Ordering numbers (page 11)

1
- a 529   595   2005   2053   2509
- b 988   1009   1023   2068   2681
- c 3740   4037   4307   4703   4730
- d 299   2894   2911   2990   3006
- e 1665   3098   3452   6112   6121

2
3458   3485   3548   3584   3845
3854   4358   4385   4538   4583
4835   4853   5348   5384   5438
5483   5834   5843   8345   8354
8435   8453   8534   8543

Unit 7: Odd and even numbers (page 12)

1 21

2
- a 141   145
- b 212   214
- c 445   441   435
- d 804   800   798

3
- a ✓   b ✗   c ✗
- d ✓   e ✓   f ✗

Unit 8: Multiples (page 13)

1 multiples of 2:   74   60   92
150   88   130   28   90   36

58

multiples of 5: 225 60 35
150 95 130 45 90 75
multiples of 10: 60 150 130 90
multiples of 2, 5 and 10: 60 150 130 90

❷ Check that all multiples of 2 are coloured, all multiples of 5 are circled.
The multiples of 10 (multiples of 2 and 5) are both circled and coloured.

Unit 9: Fractions (page 14)

❶ a $\frac{2}{3}$ b $\frac{7}{10}$ c $\frac{3}{5}$
   d $\frac{3}{10}$ e $\frac{3}{8}$ f $\frac{4}{5}$

❷ a $\frac{2}{3}$ b $\frac{4}{10}$ c $\frac{5}{5}$ or 1
   d $\frac{6}{10}$ e $\frac{4}{8}$ f $\frac{1}{5}$

Unit 10: Equivalent fractions (page 15)

❶ a $\frac{1}{4}=\frac{2}{8}$ b $\frac{1}{2}=\frac{6}{12}$ c $\frac{1}{3}=\frac{2}{6}$
   d $\frac{3}{4}=\frac{6}{8}$ e $\frac{1}{5}=\frac{2}{10}$ f $\frac{1}{4}=\frac{3}{12}$

❷ a 4 6 4 5 12
   b 6 3 12 15 6
   c 2 12 16 5 24
   d 2 15 4 25 30

Unit 11: Addition and subtraction facts (page 16)

❶ a 6+8=14   8+6=14
     14−8=6   14−6=8
   b 8+9=17   9+8=17
     17−9=8   17−8=9
   c 6+3=9   3+6=9
     9−3=6   9−6=3
   d 5+7=12   7+5=12
     12−7=5   12−5=7

❷ a 11 b 13 c 16 d 11
   e 13 f 13 g 9   h 7
   i 11 j 3   k 9   l 9

Unit 12: Function machines (page 17)

❶ a IN   7 4 11 12 14 9
     OUT 15 12 19 20 22 17
   b IN   5 6 8 12 15 9
     OUT 14 15 17 21 24 18
   c IN   14 15 18 12 15 21
     OUT 7 8 11 5 8 14
   d IN   20 18 17 24 25 26
     OUT 8 6 5 12 13 14

❷   IN 6 15 18 10 12 2
    OUT 5 14 17 9 11 1

Unit 13: Mental addition (page 18)

❶ a 71   b 127 c 75
   d 94   e 81   f 74

❷ a 65 / 33 32 / 19 14 18
   b 78 / 41 37 / 19 22 15
   c 88 / 45 43 / 28 17 26
   d 83 / 40 43 / 19 21 22
   e 91 / 52 39 / 29 23 16
   f 93 / 42 51 / 17 25 26

Unit 14: Addition patterns (page 19)

❶ a 13 130 1300   b 19 190 1900
   c 25 250 2500 d 31 310 3100
   e 24 240 243   f 23 230 235
   g 21 210 216   h 22 220 229

❷ 2100 2500 270 1580
  205 2200 250
  DECAGON   10 sides

Unit 15: Finding the difference (page 20)

❶ a 17 b 16 c 17 d 33
   e 27 f 26 g 28 h 22

❷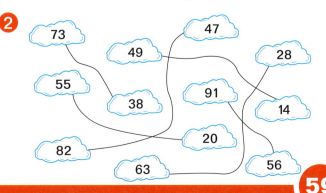

Unit 16: Mental subtraction (page 21)

1 a 27 b 17 c 22 d 8 e 37
f 26 g 24 h 27

2 $53 - 28 \rightarrow 25$ $86 - 41 \rightarrow 45$
$49 - 34 \rightarrow 15$ $62 - 47 \rightarrow 15$
$71 - 26 \rightarrow 45$ $77 - 52 \rightarrow 25$
$64 - 19 \rightarrow 45$
Check that the subtraction has an answer of 35.

Unit 17: Using brackets (page 22)

1 a 13 3 b 12 4 c 13 3
d 6 12 e 13 1

2 a $(16-10) +6$ b $13 - (6-5)$
c $(19-12) +5$ d $(24-6) - 6$
e $24 - (10+2)$

3 a 6 b 4 c 3 d 7 e 5

Unit 18: Multiplication facts (page 23)

1 a 21 b 20 c 18 d 18
80 36 27 35
16 28 24 42
9 36 40 24
33 30 40 32

2 a 2 7 b 2 9 c 4 7
8 5 6 9 9 3

Unit 19: Doubling (page 24)

1 a 50 98 38 68
b 82 54 76 52
c 74 92 560 340
d 700 840 580 360
e 420 960 780 940

2 a IN 460 450 180 320 270 260
OUT 920 900 360 640 540 520
b IN 1700 3600 4900 2300 2600 4700
OUT 3400 7200 9800 4600 5200 9400

Unit 20: Mixed calculations (page 25)

1 a 20 b 7 c 11 d 18
e 27 f 10 g 18 h 21

2 a 9 b 7 3 c 8
d 4 5 e 6 f 2 1

Unit 21: Division (page 26)

1 a 5 b 4 c 3 d 6
8 8 6 7
5 9 7 6
3 10 9 18
8 5 4 6

2 a MARS b MERCURY c SATURN

Unit 22: Division and remainders (page 27)

1 a 12 r 1 b 10 r 2 c 25 r 1
d 13 r 2 e 11 r 3 f 9 r 1
g 31 r 1 h 7 r 1 i 12 r 2
j 24 r 2 k 15 r 1 l 23 r 1
m 24 r 1 n 28 r 2 o 14 r 4

2 $50 \div 4 \rightarrow r\ 2$ $63 \div 6 \rightarrow r\ 3$
$87 \div 8 \rightarrow r\ 7$ $89 \div 10 \rightarrow r\ 9$
$74 \div 5 \rightarrow r\ 4$ $80 \div 9 \rightarrow r\ 8$
$37 \div 3 \rightarrow r\ 1$ $54 \div 7 \rightarrow r\ 5$
Make sure that the division has a remainder of 6.

Unit 23: Money (page 28)

1 a 250p b 305p c 185p
d 263p e 92p f 317p

2 a £3.70 b £2.05 c £5.65
d £1.09 e £3.42 f £0.87

3 There is more than one answer for each question. Check that the coins total the correct amount.
These are possible solutions:
a £1, 5p coins
b £1, 10p, 5p, 2p, 2p coins

c £1, 50p, 20p, 10p, 5p, 2p, 2p coins
d 50p, 20p, 10p, 5p, 2p coins
e £1, £1, 10p, 5p coins

Unit 24: Money calculations (page 29)

1 a £6.90   b £9.10   c £11.50
   d £13.10 e £8.20   f £13.10
   g £10.20 h £18.60

2 a £2.70   b £2.40   c £5.60
   d £1.70   e £1.80   f £1.70

3 a £20.40 b £3.60
   c Theme Park and Theatre

Unit 25: Mixed problems (page 30)

1 a 12 more   b 25 left
   c 9 each   d 160 g
   e 10   f 5

2 a 40 b 6 c 24 d 25 e 16

Unit 26: Mixed puzzles (page 31)

1
```
4—5—3
|   |
6 7 8
|   |
2—9—1
```

2 7+2+6   9+1+5   3+4+8
   (or any other correct answers)

3 a 38 + 53 = 91   b 86 − 49 = 37
   c 47 × 2 = 94   d 27 ÷ 3 = 9

Unit 27: 2D shapes (page 32)

1 a pentagon
   b square
   c equilateral triangle
   d octagon
   e triangle
   f pentagon
   g hexagon
   h parallelogram
   a, b, c and d are regular polygons.

2 a
All quadrilaterals have 4 sides.

b
All hexagons have 6 sides.

c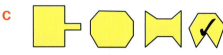
All octagons have 8 sides.

Unit 28: Symmetry (page 33)

1
a   b   c

d   e   f

2
a   b   c

3 lines of symmetry   5 lines of symmetry   6 lines of symmetry

d   e

7 lines of symmetry   8 lines of symmetry

f There are the same number of lines of symmetry as there are sides on a regular shape.

Unit 29: Naming 3D solids (page 34)

1 a → prism   b → cone
   c → cuboid   d → cylinder
   e → pyramid

61

1
a pyramid (or tetrahedron)
b cuboid
c cube
d sphere

Unit 30: Properties of 3D solids (page 35)

2

a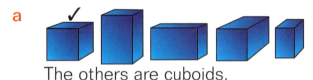
The others are cuboids.

b
The others are cylinders.

c
The others are prisms.

d
The others are pyramids.

e
The others are spheres.

2
a 1 square face and 4 triangle faces
b 2 square faces and 4 rectangle faces
c 2 triangle faces and 3 rectangle faces
d 4 triangle faces

Unit 31: Angles (page 36)

1 a 90° b 180° c 45°

2 a E S NE b N SE W
c E S NE d S NW E

Unit 32: Coordinates (page 37)

1 a house (1, 6)   pond (8, 4)
horse (3, 2)   tree (2, 7)
b (4, 8) (duck)   (2, 3) (train)
(9, 4) (tractor)   (1, 6) (house)
c (4, 4) (5, 7) (7, 0)

2 rectangle

Unit 33: Measuring length (page 38)

1 a 3 km   b 9 km   c 8000 m
d 10 m   e 4 m   f 700 cm
g 1500 cm   h 11 000 m

2 a 6 km   Bexby
b 12 km   Eastly
c 20 km   Fardon
d 10 km   Coalthorpe
e 18 km   Denton

Unit 34: Measuring mass (page 39)

1 a 3 kg   b $2\frac{1}{4}$ kg
c $5\frac{1}{2}$ kg   d $3\frac{1}{10}$ kg
e 1000 g   f 3500 g
g 10 000 g   h 2100 g

2 a $3\frac{1}{2}$ kg   b 2 kg
c $\frac{1}{2}$ kg   d 4 kg
e 72 kg   f 57 kg
g 34 kg   h 65 kg
i 250 g   j 400 g
k 650 g   l 750 g

Unit 35: Measuring capacity (page 40)

1 a 4 litres   b 2500 ml   c $1\frac{1}{2}$ litres
d 1750 ml   e $5\frac{1}{4}$ litres   f 10 000 ml
g $2\frac{1}{10}$ litres   h 4100 ml

2 a 100 ml   b 250 ml   c 500 ml
d 750 ml   e $\frac{1}{2}$ litre   f 1 litre
g $1\frac{1}{2}$ litres   h $1\frac{1}{4}$ litres   i $1\frac{1}{2}$ litres
j $3\frac{1}{2}$ litres   k $2\frac{1}{4}$ litres   l $\frac{3}{4}$ litre

Unit 36: Perimeter (page 41)

1   **a** 12 cm   **b** 14 cm   **c** 10 cm
    d 20 cm   **e** 18 cm

2   **a** 12 cm   **b** 10 cm   **c** 10 cm
    d 8 cm

Unit 37: Time (page 42)

1   **a** 4:17   **b** 9:28   **c** 6:03   **d** 3:49
    e 8:17   **f** 11:33   **g** 5:57   **h** 10:32

2   **a** 45 minutes   **b** 50 minutes
    c 30 minutes   **d** 45 minutes
    e 70 minutes   **f** 130 minutes

Unit 38: Calendars (page 43)

1   **a** January, February, October
    b February, March, November
    c 31
    d 4

2   **a** 2nd Jan   6th Feb
      6th Mar   3rd Apr
      1st May   5th Jun
      3rd Jul   7th Aug
      4th Sep   2nd Oct
      6th Nov   4th Dec
    b 7 weekends
    c Leave 1st Aug   Return 8th Aug

Unit 39: Pictograms (page 44)

Between 21 and 24 birds came to the table between 1.00 p.m. and 2.00 p.m.

1   **a** 17   **b** Saturday
    c Tuesday   **d** Thursday and Friday
    e 100

2   **a** 41 and 49
    b 71 and 79
    c Approximately 30 more dogs than cats were seen. (minimum difference 22, maximum difference 38)

Unit 40: Bar charts (page 45)

There were 7 hours of sunshine on Wednesday.

1   London: Rome:
    a 3rd   **a** 13 °C
    b 11 °C   **b** 3rd
    c 5th and 6th   **c** 6th
    d 3 °C   **d** 3 °C

2   **a** 5 °C   **b** 2nd   **c** 5 °C   **d** 6th

Test 1 (pages 46 and 47)

1   **a** four thousand six hundred and seventy-three
    b two thousand and four
    c three thousand and ninety-six

2   67   63   51

3   **a** 7 km   **b** 11 000 m
    c 3 m   **d** 800 cm

4   Saturday

5   **a** 8   **b** 14   **c** 6

6 $\frac{7}{10}$

7   **a** → hexagon
    b → quadrilateral
    c → heptagon
    d → pentagon

8   **a** 8th   **b** Tuesday

9   **a** 91   **b** 74

10   34

Test 2 (pages 48 and 49)

1   4205   3205   3215

2   Shaded numbers: 1, 4, 7, 10, 13, 16, 19, 22, 25
    Circled number: 36

3   24 cm

④ 5

⑤ IN 19 16 23 21 25 30
   OUT 7 4 11 9 13 18

⑥ a 3 b 9

⑦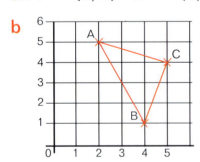

⑧ 3:32 and 6:52

⑨ a 160 b 1600 c 240 d 244

⑩ a 24 b 29

Test 3 (pages 50 and 51)

① a 380 b 801

② $2\frac{1}{4}$ kg = 2250 g

③ a 30 b 21 c 16

④ a 13 b 18 c 8 d 22

⑤ a → cylinder b → pyramid
   c → prism   d → cuboid

⑥ a A → (2, 5) B → (4, 1)

b

⑦ 609 695 6095 6509 6900

⑧ a 6 b 9 c 9

⑨ 237p = £2.37

⑩ £3.20

Test 4 (pages 52 and 53)

① (28) 35 (70)✓ 87 (100)✓ (96)✓ 85✓

② $1\frac{1}{2}$ l = 1500 ml

③ IN 380 460 2600 4200
   OUT 760 920 5200 8400

④ a 18 b 6

⑤ Triangular prism

⑥ South-east

⑦ > >

⑧ a 14 r 3 b 17 r 2 c 22 r 2

⑨ a £8.30 b £2.50

⑩ a 45 + 28 = 73 b 56 − 31 = 25
   c 36 × 2 = 72

64